DIGITAL AND INFORMATION LITERACY ™

BITCOINS:
NAVIGATING
OPEN-SOURCE CURRENCY

BARBARA GOTTFRIED HOLLANDER

rosen publishing's
rosen central

New York

This book is dedicated to J. A. Shapiro. Thank you.

Published in 2015 by The Rosen Publishing Group, Inc.
29 East 21st Street, New York, NY 10010

Library of Congress Cataloging-in-Publication Data

Hollander, Barbara Gottfried.
Bitcoins: navigating open-source currency/Barbara Gottfried Hollander.—First edition.
    pages cm.—(Digital and information literacy)
Includes bibliographical references and index.
ISBN 978-1-4777-7930-9 (library bound)—ISBN 978-1-4777-7931-6 (pbk.)—
ISBN 978-1-4777-7932-3 (6-pack)
1. Money—Juvenile literature. 2. Tokens—Juvenile literature. 3. Exchange—Juvenile literature. 4. Electronic commerce—Juvenile literature. 5. Virtual reality—Economic aspects—Juvenile literature. I. Title.
HG221.5.H65 2015
332.4'2—dc23
                                                    2014011786

Manufactured in Malaysia

CONTENTS

INTRODUCTION

What do you need to buy new clothes or pay for college? What do you use to purchase a car or pay the rent on an apartment? Money, of course. Currency is used to buy things that you need and want. Money is a medium of exchange. Money is traded for goods and services, such as clothes, tuition, a car, or a place to live. It is also a store of value. Money can be put away and used later. Money means different things to different people. For example, some people may think of $1 as a new smartphone app, while others see $1 as a cup of tea. Either way, a dollar in your wallet is worth something.

Before money, people bartered. They traded their goods and services for other goods and services. Suppose you lived thousands of years ago and wanted fresh milk every day. You need a cow, but you only have chickens. To make the trade, you look for someone willing to exchange one cow for your chickens. But how many chickens are equal to a cow? How far must you travel to make the trade? What happens if your chickens become sick on your way to another town? Bartering items were often difficult to exchange, and many items were perishable, so they did not keep their value over time.

To solve these problems, people needed a currency that expressed monetary worth, was easily carried, maintained value, and was durable. For

In the mid-1950s, cowrie shell money was still in circulation in Africa. In 2014, BitX South Africa allowed users to buy, sell, store, receive, and spend bitcoins.

thousands of years, money took on different forms. The Chinese were instru-mental in the evolution of money. In 1200 BCE, the longest-used currency emerged, known as cowrie shells. In 1000 BCE, the Chinese made bronze and copper versions of these shells. They also made metal coins with holes to wear on chains. In 118 BCE, the Chinese made banknotes made of leather and then paper currency in 806 CE.

Today, the United States has paper money and coins, such as pennies, nickels, dimes, quarters, and half dollars. People also use plastic, such as debit and credit cards, to pay for goods and services. A credit card allows you to borrow spending money today and repay it later, while a debit card is linked directly to a bank account, allowing for automatic withdrawal. Credit cards emerged in the United States in the 1920s. In 1974, a Frenchman named Roland Moreno designed a circuit that became the basis for the debit card system.

Are we ready for a new currency and payment system that incorporates twenty-first-century technology? The world has answered by producing crypto-currencies made of bits and bytes. The prime example of this digital, open-source currency is called bitcoin. According to the *New Yorker* article "The Crypto-Currency" by Joshua Davis, on the evening of January 3, 2009, a man "pressed a button on his keyboard and created a new currency called bitcoin. It was all bit and no coin. There was no paper, copper, or silver—just thirty-one thousand lines of code and an announcement on the Internet." Sounds like a science-fiction story? Read on.

Chapter 1

Currency of the Future

Bitcoin is an open-source currency. It uses community currency software that you can download for free. These digital coins are sent over the Internet and stored in a virtual wallet. The wallets are either in a cloud (public, shared network) or your computer. Bitcoins are Internet cash, and the digital wallet is your virtual bank account. Bitcoins are more than a new currency. They are an international payment system that allows for transactions with the click of a button.

A New Currency?

Think about how paper money and coins solved bartering problems. Open-source currencies, such as bitcoins, solve hard cash issues. Paper money is easier to carry around than cows, but bitcoins are even easier to carry than paper money. In fact, you can carry thousands of bitcoins on a memory stick! A bitcoin is more durable and easily stored than cash. Bitcoins are also more accessible because the Internet is open twenty-four hours a day, seven days a week, and from the convenience of your cellphone, computer, or other electronic device.

In 2013, software engineer Mike Caldwell minted physical bitcoins in Sandy, Utah.

Suppose you owe your friend money for a concert ticket. You could walk to the Automated Teller Machine (ATM), put in your PIN, withdraw cash, and then repay your friend. Or you could enter your friend's address, payment amount, and send bitcoins on your cell without leaving your seat. International transactions are simple, too. According to Bitcoin.org, "Bitcoins can be transferred from Africa to Canada in ten minutes." With cash, international transactions involve exchanging one country's currency for another. But bitcoins are not tied to any country.

In 2009, the world's first bitcoin ATM appeared in Vancouver in British Columbia, Canada.

Next, think about the extra costs of making a transaction. Payments via credit card, debit card, or other means such as PayPal involve more than the buyer and the seller. For example, using a credit card requires borrowing money from a financial institution (such as a bank) and repaying it. These third parties can mean higher "extra costs." But bitcoins are just about the buyer and the seller. So these transactions usually cost less money. Bitcoin users may choose to incur extra fees, such as sending a payment with priority option.

File   Edit   View   Favorites   Tools   Help

CURRENCY OR COMMODITY

Currency or Commodity

Some investors believe that bitcoin is a commodity, not a currency. A commodity is an exchangeable good. It can be bought and sold. On foreign exchange markets, U.S. dollars, euros, and other accepted forms of currency are bought and sold every day. But these currencies have relatively stable values. They generally do not change, or fluctuate, widely. The value of bitcoins can fluctuate a lot, however. For example, in January 2013, you could buy a bitcoin for $13. In November of that year—less than a year later—that same bitcoin cost more than $1,000.

A bitcoin fits the criteria for a "good form of money." It is sturdy, easy to carry, and accessible. But the definition of money is "something generally accepted as a medium of exchange, a measure of value, or a means of payment," according to *Merriam-Webster*. To succeed as a form of money, bitcoins must be widely accepted as a "medium of exchange" over the long run. Otherwise, they will be remembered as a commodity that once made and cost investors a lot of money.

Who's in Charge?

According to the Federal Reserve Bank of New York, there were $1.2 trillion worth of U.S. paper money and coins in July 2013. The central bank in the United States, known as the Federal Reserve, controls the amount of U.S. currency in circulation. The U.S. Department of the Treasury prints money. Now think about bitcoins. The Federal Reserve does not control its supply. Its bits and bytes are not generated by the Department of Treasury.

Bitcoin users control bitcoins. They are created through a process called mining and publicly accessible via software. When things are controlled or regulated by the government, there are organized groups of people that make decisions based on strategies and goals. With bitcoins, these groups of people are the bitcoin players. Who often determines strategy and goals for this open-source currency? The answer is the invisible hand.

In the 1700s, a prominent economist named Adam Smith wrote about an invisible hand that guides the economy. He meant that people make economic decisions based on maximizing their own good (or wealth). Smith also believed that these decisions resulted in the best allocation of resources and made society better off. Bitcoin is in sync with Smith's theory. Decisions to buy and sell bitcoins are based on people wanting to maximize their own wealth—without the presence of government intervention.

Will the Real Inventor of Bitcoins Stand Up?

The inventor of the bitcoins goes by the name Satoshi Nakamoto.
For years, people have tried to discover the identity of the person or people behind this name. Some took apart the Japanese name to search for clues. *Satoshi* means "wise" or "clear-thinking." *Naka* means "inside," "medium," or "relationship." *Moto* translates as "origin" or "foundation." A *Motherboard* article, "Who Is Satoshi Nakamoto, the Creator of Bitcoin?" combined these words into "thinking clearly inside the foundation."

The bitcoin idea emerged in November 2008 with Satoshi Nakamoto's paper called "Bitcoin: A Peer-to-Peer Electronic Cash System." By April 2011, Nakamoto announced via the Internet that he had "moved on to other things." In December 2013, Satoshi Nakamoto held about $1 billion worth of bitcoins and was named "Person of the Year" by *Business Insider*. But the identity of this person is still unclear.

Newsweek claimed that Dorian Nakamoto was the bitcoin founder. In an interview with the Associated Press, Nakamoto said, "I got nothing to do with it."

Over the years, speculation has led to several possible suspects. Could Satoshi Nakamoto be any of the following people?

- Dorian Nakamoto: A March 6, 2014, *Newsweek* article cited Dorian as the creator of bitcoins, but Satoshi Nakamoto's account on P2P Foundation announced, "I am not Dorian Nakamoto."
- Michael Clear: A British graduate student of cryptography from Trinity College in Dublin (and the college's top computer science student in 2008) has been suggested, along with other Trinity College figures

Professor Donal O'Mahony, research assistant Hitesh Tewari, and student Michael Peirce. Together, these four men are called the Crypto Mano Group, or CMG.

- Jed McCaleb: Creator of bitcoin exchange Mt. Gox, developer of Ripple ("free Paypal"), and creator of eDonkey (peer-to-peer file sharing network).
- Gavin Andresen: Bitcoin project's lead developer and chief scientist on Bitcoin Foundation's board.
- Neil J. King, Charles Bry, and Vladimir Oksman: These three men filed patents for work in encryption, communication, networks, and nodes.
- Nick Szabo: Former law and economics professor at George Washington University, Szabo has an interest in decentralized currency.
- Shinichi Mochizuki: Japanese mathematician and Kyoto University lecturer.
- Vili Lehdonvirta: Economic sociologist with specialties in virtual economies and digital work.
- Martii Malmi: Finnish developer of bitcoins user interface.
- Ross William Ulbricht: Operator of illegal Internet drug market known as Silk Road.

None of these people have been confirmed as the inventor of bitcoins. According to the *Motherboard* article, when asked, "Are you Satoshi?" some suspects answered, "Even if I was, I wouldn't tell you." For now, the true identity of the bitcoin inventor must remain a mystery.

Chapter 2

Bitcoins in Action

Bitcoin is a virtual currency. You cannot hold bitcoins in your hand, but you can hold a piece of paper that unlocks a bitcoin wallet. Bitcoins can also be traded for cash at bitcoin ATMs. They come from different sources, beginning with mining.

Mining to Find the Key

The process of making new bitcoins begins when a computer or network of computers runs the bitcoin software. This

The first bitcoin ATM in Japan was imported from the United States. It opened in a Tokyo bar and restaurant called the Pink Cow.

causes new entries in the block chains (or public records of bitcoin trans-actions). New block chains create new bitcoins. Can people produce an unlimited number of this open-source currency? No, the bitcoin process is lim-ited to about twenty-one million coins. It is estimated that bitcoins will reach this level in 2140. As of March 4, 2014, there were 12.4 million bitcoins in the world.

Mining describes the process of making new bitcoins. It consists of computers crunching complex numbers. In "CNBC Explains: How to Mine Bitcoins on Your Own," Anthony Volastro compares the block chains in mining to locked boxes. Mining is the process of finding the key. Running the software locates the key and confirms the transactions. Each key comes with twenty-five new bitcoins. According to BlockChain.info, computers try about 1.8 billion times before finding the key! Mining is one way to obtain this digital currency. You can also obtain bitcoins by buying them, accepting them as payment, or giving them as gifts.

Faster, Faster!

To mine bitcoins, it's necessary to have mining software. There are many free downloadable options. In 2013, BitGazette cited the CGMiner, Bit-Miner, DiabloMiner, Poclbm, and BFGminer as the "5 best bitcoin mining soft-ware." Both individuals and groups can mine with a computer. When mining began, bitcoins were generated quickly and personal computers worked efficiently. But the bitcoin algorithm was designed to make mining harder with the creation of more bitcoins. For example, in 2014, twenty-five new bitcoins were created every ten minutes. But in 2017, the number of coins produced every ten minutes decreases by half, and this rate continues to fall every four years.

Harder mining encouraged people to turn to more sophisticated technol-ogy specifically designed for mining, such as application-specific integrated circuits (faster hardware). New hardware gets expensive. Anthony Volastro stated that "the price tag for a full mining rig—capable of discovering new

File   Edit   View   Favorites   Tools   Help

INSIDE A BITCOIN MINE

Inside a Bitcoin Mine

In the *New York Times* article "Into the Bitcoin Mines," author Nathaniel Popper takes readers inside the bitcoin mines located in Reykjanesbaer, Iceland. "To get there, you pass through a fortified gate and enter a feature-less yellow building. After checking in with a guard behind bulletproof glass, you face four more security checkpoints, including a so-called man trap that allows passage only after the door behind you has shut. This brings you to the center of the operation, a fluorescent-lit room with more than 100 whir-ring silver computers, each in a locked cabinet and each cooled by blasts of Arctic air shot up from vents in the floor."

The computers run a twenty-four-hour program aimed at discovering new coins. The program uses a very difficult algorithm (or step-by-step proce-dure to solve a problem) to find keys that unlock the bitcoins. The computers that find the keys also get the coins. It's a race for the money! Popper quotes the thirty-one-year-old founder of the company responsible for building the mining facility. "What we have here are money-printing machines," said Emmanuel Abiodun. Abiodun chose Iceland, in part because of the inexpen-sive and abundant geothermal and hydroelectric energy. Hong Kong and Washington State also have mining facilities.

bitcoins on its own—currently costs in the ballpark of $12,000." He then cites mining pools as "a way around such a hefty investment." Each member of the pool, such as the popular Slush's pool, receives a percentage of the digital currency relative to their contribution of computer power.

Dangerous Money

The mining facilities have state-of-the-art security, such as bulletproof glass, barricaded gates, and security checkpoints. But what about your bitcoins? Are they safe? Can you lose your money? Remember that bitcoins are not backed by a government or central bank. They are not insured in case of theft. And bitcoins are subject to online heists by hackers. Once gone, bitcoins are not retrievable.

In Gizmodo's "The 6 Biggest Bitcoin Heists in History," Adam Clark Estes lists the top crypto-currency thefts as of February 27, 2014:

1. Mt. Gox (short for "Magic the Gathering Online Exchange"): Users lost $436 million worth of bitcoins

This bitcoin mining data center is located on a former NATO airbase in Iceland. Relatively inexpensive electricity makes Iceland an attractive site for bitcoin mining.

2. Silk Road: Loss of $127.4 million in bitcoins
3. Sheep Marketplace: Cyber thieves got away with $56.4 million
4. Silk Road 2: Loss of $2.7 million
5. Mt. Gox: Another loss of $500,000 for this exchange

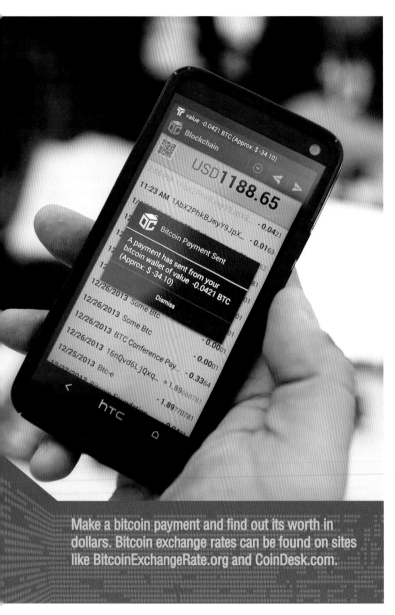

Make a bitcoin payment and find out its worth in dollars. Bitcoin exchange rates can be found on sites like BitcoinExchangeRate.org and CoinDesk.com.

Suppose that two people each have $500. One person puts her money in the bank. The other buys bitcoins. Now imagine that the bank fails and the bitcoin exchange is hacked. Like most banks, the bank is FDIC-insured. This means that the depositor still has her $500. But because bitcoins are not backed, the bitcoin user lost his or her money. Now imagine that two different people want to use their money to buy a new computer. The first person uses money from a savings account, and the other person wants to pay in bitcoins. On the day of the purchase, the value of bitcoins falls. The bank holder can still make the purchase, but the bitcoin holder may no longer have enough money for the computer.

There are different levels of risk for each form of currency and payment system. Each person has his or her own risk tolerance. Some people are more apt to engage in risky activities, such as buying bitcoins. Others like to "play it safe" and put their money in the bank. Look at bitcoins and a savings account as investments. The payoff for each investment correlates to the risk. While bitcoins are riskier, they also have a potentially bigger payoff than a savings account. You can earn more money by putting your funds in bitcoins. The flip side is that there is a greater chance of losing it.

Twenty-first-century technology offers new securities. Bitcoin transactions are protected by military-grade cryptography (process of solving codes). The cryptography that unlocks the block chains creates both a public key and a private key. Security issues arising from the actual buying and selling of goods and services with bitcoins are reduced by this cryptography. There is also less opportunity for the identity theft associated with credit cards. But this same technology introduces new challenges for the monetary world—in the form of cyber thieves stealing crypto-currency from virtual wallets.

Chapter 3

Got Bitcoin?

itcoin is an open-source currency. Virtual wallets on electronic devices hold open-source currency. Security risks inherent to the Internet pose challenges for bitcoin users. But they also create opportunities for businesses to create solutions to protect bitcoin holdings. Fluctuations in bitcoin value also create risks, but investors use arbitrage to earn profits from these fluctuations. The marketplace for bitcoins is dynamic. New factors affect the supply and demand for this currency daily.

Virtual Wallets

Bitcoins are stored in virtual-reality wallets. There are software, mobile, and web wallets. The hard drive of a computer holds the software wallet, while a mobile device (such as your cell) holds the mobile wallet. To create wallets, download the appropriate software, such as Bitcoin-Qt, MultiBit, and Hive for desktop wallet programs, or Bitcoin Wallet for Androids that runs on tablets and cells. Web wallets are found on the sites of bitcoin providers and include Coinbase and Blockchain. Coinbase offers dollar-bitcoin trading, and Blockchain had the first mobile services for both Android and iOS.

Mark Karpeles was the chief executive officer (CEO) at Mt. Gox. Residing in Japan, Karpeles did return to the United States in April 2014 as requested by a U.S. court.

All wallets pose security risks. Maybe a bitcoin wallet isn't something that could be lost when it falls out of your coat pocket, but you could lose your bitcoin wallet if your computer crashes, your cell is stolen, or your bitcoin provider site is hacked. Take precautions, such as backing up computer data, encrypting your wallet and smartphone with passwords, and using the latest versions of software. Keep updated on the latest ways to protect your bitcoins. Finally, be on the lookout for danger signs. Mt. Gox crashed twice before filing for bankruptcy.

File   Edit   View   Favorites   Tools   Help

FILL IT

Fill It

You want to fill your bitcoin wallet. According to Earn-Bitcoins.com, you have several options:

- Mine to find the key that unlocks this open-source currency.
- Accept payment in bitcoins for selling a good.
- Find a part-time job that pays in bitcoins, such as watching videos or answering online surveys.
- Lend out your bitcoins and earn bitcoin interest (money earned from loans).
- Ask your full-time employer for your salary in bitcoins.
- Trade your bitcoins for profit on an exchange.

In December 18, 2013, the federal government owned one of the biggest bitcoin wallets. After busting the online drug market called Silk Road, the FBI seized 144,000 Bitcoins, then valued at about $100 million. But this amount pales in comparison to the one million bitcoins rumored to be held by mysterious creator, Satoshi Nakamoto. His bitcoins are reportedly spread among different wallets. In his article, "Who Owns the World's Biggest Bitcoin Wallet? The FBI," Robert McMillan reports that there were 159,916 bitcoin addresses "with at least one bitcoin," in December 2012 compared to 246,377 one year later.

In the *Business Insider* article, "Here's What Happened When I Bought Bitcoin in Person," Lauren Orsini discusses how to buy this currency in person with the use of LocalBitcoins. In October 2013, LocalBitcoins was the "widest reaching peer-to-peer bitcoin exchange," with bitcoin buyers in "190 countries and 3,317 cities." This exchange connected Orsini with bitcoin seller Richard Weston.

The Bitcoin Wallet smartphone app can be downloaded on cell phones, such as the iPhone 5.

The transaction included recording Orsini's name and the amount of the trade in dollars and bitcoins. Weston confirmed Orsini's wallet address and logged into his wallet. Once Orsini paid cash, the bitcoins appeared in her web wallet. While this transaction went smoothly, face-to-face bitcoin exchanges pose risks, such as being scammed or robbed. Buyers should also take regular safety precautions when meeting with a stranger, such as choosing a public place.

Cold Storage

Cold storage is an offline wallet that provides the highest level of security. It stores your wallet in a place that is not connected to the bitcoin network, or even the Internet. The only way for someone to steal your bitcoins is to steal your offline computer and figure out your advanced wallet encryption. An offline wallet is created the same way as an online wallet. But it also includes a "watching-only" copy, which can provide receiving addresses and generate transactions.

For example, suppose you want to buy a pair of jeans on Overstock.com and pay in bitcoins. First, you jump online to create an unsigned transaction. Then, you go offline to sign it. Finally, you announce the transaction online. All three steps potentially take less than sixty seconds. According to Coinbase.com, 97 percent of Coinbase's funds are stored offline.

The wallet service Armory offers both online and offline services. To run its offline services, you need an offline computer or laptop, Armory installer, and rewritable media, such as a USB drive. However, it is not necessary to have the same operating systems for both online and offline computers. Armory allows you to manage your offline wallet. You can also make hard copies of the codes (private keys) for your wallet by printing them out or writing them on a piece of paper. Then you can store this information in a safe place, such as a safety deposit box or vault. Hard copies ensure that your wallet is always backed up.

Supply and Demand

You can trade your bitcoins on an exchange. A bitcoin exchange is a marketplace for buyers and sellers of this open-source currency. But what determines the buying and selling price of a bitcoin? There is no central monetary authority for crypto-currency, so a government or central bank does not set its value. Rather, the value of this currency is determined by the basics of economics: supply and demand.

In 2014, the D Las Vegas and the Golden Gate Hotel & Casino became the first casino property to accept bitcoin—but not for use on the gambling floors.

Supply is determined by mining, which is based on an algorithm, or a complicated set of rules for solving a problem. With regular paper and coin currency, most money is created through a process of lending though commercial banks. When banks lend money, they credit their customers' accounts with "money" to spend in the marketplace. At the end of 2013, there were few bitcoin lending sites. So the supply of bitcoins was basically the amount of mined coins.

People who want bitcoins determine the currency's demand. For example, suppose someone wants bitcoins to engage in arbitrage. "Arbitrage" refers to buying an asset at one price and quickly selling it at a higher price for profit. The investor takes this idea straight to the market and finds an online exchange. She signs up, creates a username, answers the e-mail confirmation, and provides proof of address and a photo ID issued by the government. Now, she is ready to buy and sell bitcoins. People also demand bitcoins to make payments for goods and services.

Increases in the demand for this currency can also increase its value (or price), as the amount of people demanding this currency outpaces its supply. For example, if more businesses accept bitcoins as payment, then more consumers might want their wealth held in bitcoins. As with any currency, confidence also affects demand. When people are confident in the stability of a currency, it can increase the demand for that currency. On the flip side, if people lose confidence in bitcoins, the currency's demand (and value) decreases.

Chapter 4

Bitcoin Backers

What do governments think of a borderless, open-source currency? They cannot control bitcoins with their central banks or set their exchange rates. Government regulations and protections do not apply to bitcoin users. Bitcoins are also unchartered territory for other players. Investors view them as a speculative asset used to earn profits. More businesses view them as an acceptable form of payment, whereas a growing number of consumers pay in bitcoins.

China's Mixed Response

China has been involved in the development of currency for thousands of years. Where does it stand on twenty-first-century crypto-currency? In 2009, a virtual currency called QQ (from Tencent) took off quickly in China. Within a few years, it accounted for a possible 13 percent of China's cash economy. QQ was traded in public places and accepted for transactions. The Communist Party in China was not pleased. In the article "Why China Wants to Dominate Bitcoin," Stan Stalnaker reports, "The Chinese government…[told] Tencent to limit QQ's use or face a total shutdown of their business. So Tencent reeled it in."

Bitcoin users could access virtual currency QQ with a smartphone app. QQ was offered by Tencent, a Chinese Internet service portal.

Now consider bitcoins in the year 2013, when the currency's value increased more than 6,000 percent. A company called BTC China became the world's biggest bitcoin exchange. According to the article "China Bites into Bitcoin" by Kashmir Hill, BTC China was trading "more than 100,000 of the virtual coins, or $100 million . . . on a single day." This Chinese company backed the open-source currency. China's central bank was wary, however, and responded by not allowing business owners to accept bitcoins as payment. It also forbade financial institutions from exchanging bitcoins and yuans (Chinese currency).

Think about how the Bank of China's actions decreased bitcoin demand. First, its actions decreased the use of bitcoins as a form of payment. Second, its actions made bitcoins less attractive as a medium of exchange because they could not be converted into local currency. Finally, the Bank of China made people lose confidence in this new currency. When BTC China became the world's biggest bitcoin exchange, the bitcoin's value was more than $1,100. After the Bank of China's actions, its value was less than $500.

MYTH Bitcoins are controlled by a central bank.

FACT Bitcoins are a decentralized currency.

MYTH Bitcoins are only used as an investment tool.

FACT Bitcoins are also used as payment for goods and services.

MYTH The supply of bitcoins is unlimited.

FACT The bitcoin algorithm produces about twenty-one million coins.

U.S. Dollar vs. Bitcoins

"The fact that people are hacking bitcoins really hard, it almost hearkens back to when banks first started and they didn't have safe safes and people were going into the banks and just robbing money out of the safe. It actually validates the value of the money itself," celebrity Ashton Kutcher told CNBC.com's Cadie Thompson.

Kutcher is speaking out on bitcoins, intrigued both with the crypto-currency and its decentralized technology. "People could anonymously monitor each other on the Internet for criminal behavior and this civic participation would help eliminate government intrusion," continued Kutcher. "The same infrastructure that built out bitcoin could be used in the security industry for mass good."

At one time, people questioned the stability and safety of the U.S. dollar and its banking system. When banks collapsed in the 1920s, people lost their money. Gaining confidence in the stability of the U.S. dollar and its financial system was part of a process. The banking system eventually offered increased security measures for their customers. A few years after bitcoins emerged, businesses provided cold storage.

This process is ongoing for all financial systems. During the global financial crises in the early 2000s, companies and individuals lost billions of dollars, financial institutions closed, stock markets crashed, and countries' economies stopped growing. Many Americans once again lost confidence in the U.S financial system. Attempts at rebuilding and increased regulations are still underway. In the bitcoin world, confidence can also be shaken by crashes in bitcoin exchanges. Such is the nature of the financial world.

Accept It

A growing number of businesses are accepting bitcoins as payment. This increases its use as a medium of exchange and strengthens its validity as

Bitcoin security platform, BitGo, raised millions of dollars in Series A funding from investors, such as Ashton Kutcher.

a form of currency. Popular businesses that accept bitcoins for payment include the following:

- **Overstock.com** In January 2013, Overstock.com became one of the biggest retailers to accept this open-source currency.
- **TigerDirect.com** This is another popular online retailer that accepts bitcoins.
- **Amazon.com** Shop for books, movies, and more with online currency.
- **Home Depot** Home improvements can be paid for in bitcoins.
- **CVS** Pay for drugstore purchases with virtual currency.
- **Kmart** This brick-and-mortar store accepts cryptocurrency.
- **Sears** This store is another brick-and-mortar supporting the bitcoin revolution.
- **Zynga** Pay for games, such as FarmVille 2, CastleVille, and CityVille, from this mobile gaming company with bitcoins.
- **Virgin Galactic** This aviation company will fly you into space in exchange for virtual currency.
- **OkCupid** Use bitcoins to pay for this online dating service.
- **WordPress** This social media platform is used by companies such as the *New York Times*, CNN, Reuters, and Mashable.
- **Subway** Order a sub in the Allentown, Pennsylvania, location and pay in bitcoins.
- **Lumfile** This file server is cloud-based and accepts bitcoins.
- **Pizza for Coins** Order pizza from Domino's with funds from your virtual wallet.
- **World Aid for Homeless Children** Make a bitcoin donation.

Chapter 5

Will the Bubble Burst?

Investors may view bitcoins as a speculative asset. It is something of value that carries large risk and tremendous potential profit. Throughout history, speculative bubbles have burst, resulting in fast and large drops in an asset's value and millions of dollars in losses. These bubbles have included assets, such as houses. Will a bitcoin bubble burst? Or will bitcoin survive as a viable currency? And how will governments respond?

Bitcoin Regulation Controversy

Government regulations are rules that govern behavior. They are enforceable by law. On January 31, 2014, the Verge posted an article called "U.S. Treasury Confirms Bitcoin Miners and Investors Won't Be Regulated." On February 26, 2014, NYTimes.com posted an article called "Now, Nations Mull the Ways to Regulate Bitcoin." What happened?

Just as the financial crises that began in 2007 caused governments to think about reforms for the financial system, both the collapse of Mt. Gox and Silk Road prompted conversation about possible bitcoin regulations. In

File   Edit   View   Favorites   Tools   Help

MORE CRYPTO-CURRENCIES

More Crypto-Currencies

Bitcoin is the biggest open-source currency, and its popularity has inspired the emergence of other crypto-currencies. Any successful new product offers something different than its existing competitors. How do other crypto-currencies compare with bitcoins?

- Litecoins are adequately mined with only consumer-grade hardware, have faster transactions, and a limited supply of 84 million.
- Ripple offers a system of crypto-currency, payment network, and distributed exchange. It also has major investors, such as Andreessen Horowitz, Google Ventures, and Lightspeed Venture Partners.
- Peercoin uses less energy for mining (environmentally friendly), increased security, and is technically unlimited (potential advantage for currency, disadvantage for investment).
- Primecoin uses prime numbers for encryption basis.
- QuarkCoin offers a high level of security to the tune of nine rounds of encryption and six algorithms.

"Bitcoin Regulation Coming This Year," Jose Pagliery wrote, "Benjamin Lawsky, New York's financial services superintendent, said he will issue BitLicenses' to companies dealing with bitcoins. That would mark the most significant step thus far in the United States to regulate the digital currency."

The locations of bitcoin ATMs have also been influenced by regulations. In the article, "How an Underdog Won the Race to Bring Bitcoin ATMs to the U.S.," Fran Berkman reports, "The current situation in New York does not favor any operator in bitcoin. The regulations are very restrictive on creating new [bitcoin] businesses." New Mexico and Massachusetts both have bitcoin ATMs, with Texas and California set to follow. Bitcoin ATM

Traders protest their losses in front of the Mt. Gox office. In June 2014, the bitcoin exchange Mt. Gox won approval for Chapter 15 bankruptcy protection from a U.S. court.

operators are required to register with the Financial Crimes Enforcement Network of the Treasury Department.

In February 2014, Senator Joe Manchin of West Virginia also called for a ban (or at least, strict regulations) on bitcoin. He cited its questionable uses and unstable value. Chairwoman Janet Yellen of the Federal Reserve reiterated that the Federal Reserve cannot regulate bitcoin. The controversy over regulating this inherently free market currency continues.

Federal Reserve Chairwoman Janet Yellen noted that bitcoin operates outside the domains of the banking system.

Silk Road

"Silk Road" refers to an Internet market for drugs and other illegal goods. Bitcoins was the currency of choice for Silk Road because of its anonymous online transaction capabilities. In October 2013, the Federal Bureau of Investigation took millions in bitcoins from alleged twenty-nine-year-old Silk Road operator Ross William Ulbricht. Nicknamed "Dread Pirate Roberts," Ulbricht was indicted by a grand jury in a Manhattan federal court in February 2014. He was charged with trafficking drugs, hacking computers, and money laundering. He was expected to plead not guilty.

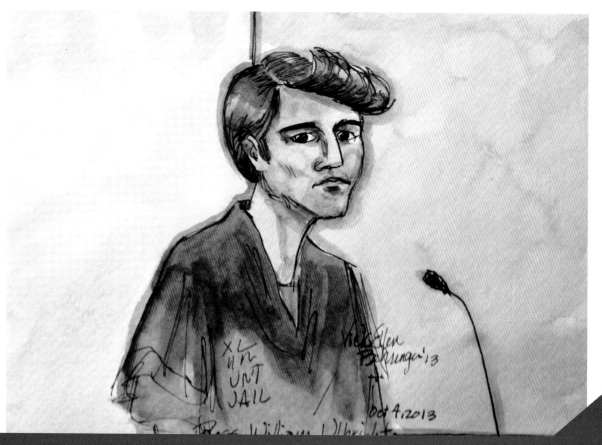

Ross William Ulbricht appeared at Federal Court in San Francisco for his alleged participation in Silk Road.

In "Meet Ross Ulbricht, the Man Charged with Running the 'Amazon.com of Drugs,' Silk Road," Joe Coscarelli cites the Southern District of New York's federal complaint: "Silk Road enable[ed] 'several thousand drug dealers' to move 'hundreds of kilograms of illegal drugs.' The site's sales totaled about $1.2 billion in the form of 9.5 million bitcoins…About $3.6 million in the Internet currency has been seized."

In January 2014, Charlie Shrem was also arrested for illegal activities connected to Silk Road. He was the chief executive officer of a bitcoin exchange known as BitInstant and vice chairman of the Bitcoin Foundation. The Justice Department claimed Robert M. Faiella used BitInstant to fill bitcoin orders. Then, he supposedly made money by selling them to Silk Road users.

Bitcoin users can buy the currency at bitcoin ATMs. In 2014, the Internal Revenue Service (IRS) viewed bitcoin as property for federal tax purposes.

Shrem and Faiella were each charged with operating a money transmitting business without a license and conspiracy to commit money laundering.

Bitcoins Around the World

The popularity of bitcoins has encouraged some countries, such as China, to take a strong stance. Security and Governmental Affairs Committee Chairman Senator Tom Carper from Delaware delegated the job of asking forty countries for their bitcoin opinions to the Law Library of Congress. Countries had mixed reactions. For example, Brazil passed a law in October 2013 in support of electronic currencies, whereas Denmark denounced bitcoins as a currency.

The survey also addressed taxes and currency recognition. Countries issuing tax guidance on bitcoins include Canada, Germany, and Singapore. Israel, Ireland, Poland, and Australia are considering plans to tax. Argentina and Croatia were among the nations that did not view bitcoins as a legal currency. And many countries, such as the United States, issued warnings about the risks and potential illegal uses of bitcoins.

While some governments do not support bitcoins, the currency continues to gain popularity. More companies accept bitcoin payments and the currency's value encourages investing. To become a widely accepted legal tender, bitcoins must be sustainable. Their value may have dropped from more than $1,000 to less than $500 after the Bank of China's 2013 actions, but it bounced back to over $1,000 on U.S. exchanges several weeks later.

GLOSSARY

algorithm Complicated set of rules for solving a problem.

arbitrage Buying an asset for one price and selling it quickly for a higher price to earn profit.

bit An element of computer information expressed as 0 or 1.

bitcoin Virtual or digital currency that employs peer-to-peer technology; it uses community software and cryptography for security.

block chain Public record of bitcoin transactions.

byte Equal to eight bits of computer information.

cold storage Offline wallet that provides high security.

commodity Exchangeable good.

cryptocurrency Money that uses cryptography for security.

cryptography Protecting information by encrypting it into a text that is deciphered with a key; bitcoin uses public and private keys.

decentralized market Structure that allows investors to buy and sell without a central place.

encryption Information changed from one form to another, often to change its meaning.

market exchange Market where participants buy and sell assets.

mining Process of making new bitcoins.

money Something that can be used as a medium of exchange, stores value, and serves as payment for goods and services.

open-source currency Money that uses community currency software.

regulation Rules that govern behavior.

risk Chance that something will turn out differently than expected.

speculative bubble When an asset's price increases more than normal economic conditions can explain.

FOR MORE INFORMATION

Bank of Canada
234 Wellington Street
Ottawa, ON K1A 0G9
Canada
(613) 782-8111
Website: http://www.bankofcanada.ca
As the central bank of Canada, it maintains the value of the Canadian dollar.

Board of Governors of the Federal Reserve System
Twentieth Street and Constitution Avenue NW
Washington, DC 20551
Website: http://www.federalreserve.gov
The United States' central bank influences the country's money supply through
    open-market operations.

Canada Revenue Agency
Office of the Minister of National Revenue
555 MacKenzie Avenue, 7th Floor
Ottawa, ON K1A 0L5
Canada
(800) 267-6999
Website: http://www.cra-arc.gc.ca
The Canada Revenue Agency carries out the tax laws for the government of
    Canada and most provinces and territories.

Department of the Treasury
1500 Pennsylvania Avenue NW
Washington, DC 20220
(202) 622-2000

Website: http://www.treasury.gov
The Financial Crimes Enforcement Network (FinCEN) is part of the U.S.
 Department of Treasury. The FinCEN handles financial crimes, like
 domestic and international money laundering.

Internal Revenue Service (IRS)
U.S. Department of Treasury
1500 Pennsylvania Avenue NW
Washington, DC 20220
(800) 829-1040
Website: http://www.irs.gov
The IRS is a government agency that collects taxes, including those imposed
 on certain investments.

U.S. Securities and Exchange Commission
100 F Street NE
Washington, DC 20549
(202) 942-8088
Website: http://www.sec.gov
SEC's protects investors and promotes fair and efficient markets.

Websites

Because of the changing nature of Internet links, Rosen Publishing has
developed an online list of websites related to the subject of this book. This
site is updated regularly. Please use this link to access the list:

http://www.rosenlinks.com/DIL/Bitc

FOR FURTHER READING

Anderson, Brandon. *The Bitcoin Revolution: The History, Mystery, and What It ALL Means!* www.VyralStart.com, 2014. Kindle edition.

Branson, Elliott. *Bitcoin: The Ultimate Beginner's Guide for Understanding Bitcoins and What You Need to Know.* Kindle ed. Seattle, WA: Amazon Digital Services, 2014.

Carroll, Richard. *Bitcoin Secrets Revealed: The Complete Bitcoin Guide—Buying, Selling, Mining, Investing and Exchange Trading in Bitcoin.* Kindle ed. Seattle, WA: Amazon Digital Services, 2014.

Guttmann, Benjamin. *The Bitcoin Bible.* Norderstedt, Germany: Books on Demand, 2013.

Jeffrey, Mark. *Bitcoin Explained Simply: An Easy Guide to the Basics That Anyone Can Understand.* Kindle ed. Los Angeles, CA: Mark Jeffrey, 2014.

Patterson, Sam. *Bitcoin Beginner: A Step by Step Guide to Buying, Selling and Investing in Bitcoins.* Kindle ed. Charleston, WV: Better Life Publishers, 2013.

Rivenburgh, Kris. *Bitcoin Made Easy: The Easiest Guide to Bitcoin You Will Ever Read.* Dallas, TX: Rivenburgh Publishing, 2013.

Smithers, A. H. *Everything You Need to Know About Buying, Selling, and Investing in Bitcoin.* Vol. 2. Seattle, WA: CreateSpace Independent Publishing Platform, 2013.

Wilcox, Devon. *Bitcoin Beginner's Guide: Everything You Need to Know to Become Rich with Bitcoins.* Kindle ed. Clydebank Publishing, 2014.

BIBLIOGRAPHY

Albrecht, Radoslav. "Bitcoin Money Supply and Money Creation." *DGC*, September 17, 2013. Retrieved February 2014 (http://www.dgcmagazine.com/bitcoin-money-supply-and-money-creation).

Armory. "Using Our Wallet." Retrieved February 2014 (https://bitcoinarmory.com/about/using-our-wallet).

Berkman, Fran. "How an Underdog Won the Race to Bring Bitcoin ATMs to the U.S." Mashable, February 25, 2014. Retrieved March 2014 (http://mashable.com/2014/02/25/bitcoin-atm-new-york).

Bitcoin.org. Retrieved February 2014 (https://bitcoin.org/en).

Bitgazette. "The 5 Best Bitcoin Mining Software." August 11, 2013. Retrieved February 2014 (http://www.bitgazette.com/article/the-5-best-bitcoin-mining-software).

BlockChain. Retrieved February 2014 (http://blockchain.info).

CoinDesk. 2014. Retrieved February 2014 (http://www.coindesk.com).

Coscarelli, Joe. "Meet Ross Ulbricht, the Man Charged with Running the 'Amazon.com of Drugs,' Silk Road." *New York Magazine*, October 2, 2013. Retrieved March 2014 (http://nymag.com/daily/intelligencer/2013/10/ross-ulbricht-charged-with-running-silk-road.html).

Davis, Joshua. "The Crypto-Currency." *New Yorker*, October 10, 2011. Retrieved February 2014 (http://www.newyorker.com/reporting/2011/10/10/111010fa_fact_davis).

Earn Bitcoins. "Earn Bitcoins in 8 Different Ways." 2013. Retrieved February 2014 (http://earn-bitcoins.com).

Estes, Adam Clark. "The 6 Biggest Bitcoin Heists in History." Gizmodo, February 27, 2014. Retrieved February 2014 (http://gizmodo.com/the-6-biggest-bitcoin-heists-in-history-1531881137).

Fuller, Cameron. "Bitcoin Around the World: How Virtual Currencies Are Treated in 40 Different Countries." *International Business Times*, February 5, 2014. Retrieved March 2014 (http://www.ibtimes.com/

bitcoin-around-world-how-virtual-currencies-are-treated-40-different
-countries-1553532).

Hill, Kashmir. "China Bites into Bitcoins." *Forbes*, January 6, 2014. Retrieved February 2014 (http://www.forbes.com/sites/kashmirhill/2014/01/06/china-bites-into-bitcoin).

Kar, Ian. "What Companies Accept Bitcoins?" NASDAQ, February 2, 2014. Retrieved February 2014 (http://www.nasdaq.com/article/what-companies-accept-bitcoin-cm323438).

Liu, Alec. "Who Is Satoshi Nakamoto, the Creator of Bitcoin?" *Motherboard*, May 22, 2013. Retrieved February 2014 (http://motherboard.vice.com/blog/who-is-satoshi-nakamoto-the-creator-of-bitcoin).

McMillan, Robert. "Who Owns the World's Biggest Bitcoin Wallet? The FBI." *Wired*, December 18, 2013. Retrieved February 2014 (http://www.wired.com/wiredenterprise/2013/12/fbi_wallet).

O'Brien, Chris. "Leading Bitcoin Exec Charged in Silk Road Money Laundering Scheme." *Los Angeles Times*, January 27, 2014. Retrieved March 2014 (http://articles.latimes.com/2014/jan/27/business/la-fi-tn-bitcoin-exchangers-arrested-in-silk-road-money-laundering-scheme-20140127).

Orsini, Lauren. "Here's What Happened When I Bought Bitcoin in Person." *Business Insider*, October 23, 2013. Retrieved February 2014 (http://www.businessinsider.com/heres-what-happened-when-i-bought-bitcoin-in-person-2013-10).

Stalnaker, Stan. "Why China Wants to Dominate Bitcoin?" CNN.com, November 18, 2013. Retrieved March 2014 (http://money.cnn.com/2013/11/18/investing/bitcoin-china).

Thompson, Cadie. "Ashton Kutcher Bites into 'Bitcoin Revolution.'" CNBC.com, May 1, 2013. Retrieved March 2014 (http://www.cnbc.com/id/100696230).

INDEX

About the Author

Barbara Gottfried Hollander has authored several economics books, including *How Currency Devaluation Works*; *How Credit Crises Happen*; *Money Matters: An Introduction to Economics*; and *Booms, Bubbles, and Busts: The Economic Cycle*. She was the economics editor of the *World Almanac and Book of Facts* and an author with the Council for Economic Education. She received a B.A. in economics from the University of Michigan and an M.A. in economics from New York University, specializing in statistics and econometrics and international economics.

Photo Credits

Cover and p. 1 (left) © iStockphoto.com/Photo-Dave; cover and p. 1 (center left) © iStockphoto.com/Eraxion; cover and p. 1 (center right) © iStockphoto.com/merznatalia; cover and p. 1 (right), p. 8 George Frey/ Getty Images; p. 5 Matthew Chattle/Dorling Kindersley/Getty Images; p. 9 David Ryder/Getty Images; pp. 12, 35, 37 © AP Images; p. 14 Jiji Press/ AFP/Getty Images; p. 17 Richard Perry/The New York Times/Redux; p. 18 Joe Raedle/Getty Images; pp. 21, 23, 28 Bloomberg/Getty Images; p. 25 Ethan Miller/Getty Images; p. 31 John Lamparski/WireImage/Getty Images; p. 36 Mark Wilson/Getty Images; p. 38 The Washington Post/Getty Images; cover and interior pages (dots graphic) © iStockphoto.com/suprun; interior pages (browser window graphic) © iStockphoto.com/AF-studio.

Designer: Nicole Russo; Editor: Heather Moore Niver;
Photo Researcher: Karen Huang